50/50

50/50

Poems by

Julianne Palumbo

Copyright©2018 Julianne Palumbo
All Rights Reserved
Published by Unsolicited Press

No part of this book may be reproduced or transmitted in any form or by any means without written permission from the publisher or author.

Printed in the United States of America.

Attention schools and businesses: for discounted copies on large orders, please contact the publisher directly.

ISBN: 978-1-947021-50-1

TABLE OF CONTENTS

One-by-One	8
On Turning Fifty	9
Something Borrowed	10
Cleaning Day	12
Sunset	13
The Scale	15
Faded Memories	17
To My Childhood Friend on Your Wedding Day	18
Grown Children	19
Fifty Something	21
Knowing Prayer	22
Fibromyalgia	24
On the morning of your wedding	25
Making Alfredo	27
Vintage Beach Scene at Watch Hill, RI	29
When Their Sister Left For College	30
Things a Mother Pulls from Her Purse	31
Some June Nights	33
Seventeen	34
Far from the Nest	35
The Swing of Young Adulthood	37
Writer's Block	39
The Afterimage	41
If we could just dance	42
About the Author	45
Acknowledgements	46

50/50

ONE-BY-ONE

We paired well
two by two by two
until you started leaving
one by one.

Now my count to three
brings me to scattered places
while leaving bodies on the couch
mismatched like laundered socks
or that bed-hidden slipper.

Now, more like those pairs
that aren't—
a pair of jeans
a pair of glasses
a pair of scissors—
a pair that makes one not two.

One headlight
will not show the way;
one wiper will not
clear the rain.
A single chopstick
or even three
cannot pick up
rice.

ON TURNING FIFTY

Fifty finds me
impaled
on a white picket fence,
stuck in the quicksand
of comfort and habit,
choking on the syllables of routine,
and leaves me
looking backward to measure
my worth in the
teaspoons used for cooking
five different meals
for five different people
and looking forward
but too nearsighted to see
my next step,
the one
that will need to matter
somehow
as much as all
the last.

SOMETHING BORROWED

"Do you mind?" she says,
through her daisy smile.
She drops her folded arms
to show me the clothes she is borrowing
and flashes me those green eyes
her younger brother says
would be big for a cow.

"Go ahead," I say.

She disappears with my new jeans
into her den of a room
where shirts and shoes
and other unsuspecting items
fall prey to wanton clutter.
I smile and shut my closet light,
content to keep my new riding boots
for now.

Years ago she borrowed my body,
my blood, my nourishment,
even my air.
They filled her like rain-soaked soil
fills a fledgling sprout,
and grew her strong and ready.
I poured thick into her
my time, my attention, my teaching.
Love.

The other day she borrowed my words,
threatening to sing opera to her young cousin
if he didn't settle down.

The memory giggled inside me
for the countless times I promised
and followed through,
crooning high notes
and made-up words
above the discord of sibling squabble
until their fighting words joined in harmony
to silence me.

My heart wavers now between
the syrup of flattery and
the elixir of thankfulness
that still, in the vibrancy of her youth,
she finds appeal
in the clothes I wear,
in the things I say,
in the love I have to offer.

There's so much more
I hope to lend.

CLEANING DAY

On Saturdays
Mom would tear rags
from Papa's white Tees.
She'd make a small snip
through the crew neck
then pull in both directions
elbows out
until the shirt gave,
cracked down the center,
and blew dust into the sunbeam light.

We'd wait for rag and bucket
before she sent us off
each in our own direction
to scrub the dirt
that caked our path
to the day's freedom.

Now as I lean over my kitchen table,
fold cloths into brisk piles,
I think of you, my sisters,
in your separate places,
and I feel that pull
in both directions,
and then that crack down my center,
sending bits of my fibers
all the way back home.

SUNSET

Fifty catches you
off guard,
like a bright morning
after a deep sleep.
Like a purse snatcher,
it sneaks up
silently
but with purpose.

Fifty raises questions,
causes you to life look,
makes you wish you were
the sun
or
a tree.

You rationalize.
Sunsets can be long,
dazzling,
memorable.
Old trees continue
to bear fruit
and weight.
Their age and size
makes them stronger,
more rooted.

Someone writes that
50 is the new 30,
and you decide to believe it
until you decide it
means nothing.

Then suddenly
you realize you cannot
fight it.
It's going to happen
anyway.
You come to accept it
and to embrace it,
to forgive yourself
for questioning.

You decide to
act your age,
hoping all the while
you might
look younger.

You begin to focus less on
what you've done
and more on what you haven't
but still intend to do.

The sun rises again.
You notice it now,
every time,
and feel more grateful.

THE SCALE

Numbers lie
like biased media
or propagandized prose.
They inflate
and deflate.
A politician's resume.

The nurse points to the scale.
I point to my shoes.
"Step on," she says.
"I'll take those into account."
I can only stare at the box
that will betray me.

The weights tip overboard.
She offers me 2 lbs.
I start the negotiation much higher.
"I'll take ten," I say.
She chuckles but holds her cards.
Two it is.

I mumble about how I started a diet today,
while judgment burns in my patient file.

When I get home,
I take the shoes,
belt,
pants,
sweater,
and pile them high
on my scale, dusty in the corner.
I shake the dice

and hope for high numbers
this time.

Her bets were off,
but not as far as mine.
The scale settles the score
somewhere in the middle,
somewhere too close
to home.

FADED MEMORIES

Some days,
pearly memories
of my children's childhood
glow behind my mind's curtain
like spirits watching me.

Lustrous,
nacreous,
gems made inside the body,
beauty beyond hard offerings
of earth.

The lull of their coo and hmmm
repeating,
repeating like the soft trumpet of a conch,
phantom puffs of their breath
caressing with the tickle of a tropical breeze,
the salty scent of their most delicate shell
releasing the warmth of the sun.

I can almost, almost...

Some days
I stand knee deep in crystal water,
the sun shimmering a faux jewel
beneath my feet.

I reach in
to grab for it,
wanting it all back,
but my hand simply ends up wet.

TO MY CHILDHOOD FRIEND ON YOUR WEDDING DAY

It isn't the long chats
or the homework
at my desk
or milk and Russian tea cakes
the colors of Easter.

It isn't the Friday night shows
the braided hair
the pizza-making
or the rants about everyone
else.

It isn't the music we danced to,
our favorite books,
our poodle hair, or
our wide-legged pants.

It's my mother
the way she treated you
as her own,
always suggesting
more lipstick.
It's this
that you remember
on your wedding day
thirty years later.

GROWN CHILDREN

Like an eyelash
curled between my fingertips,
those pastel stroller days
slipped away.

Pinked sky rippled
into autumn toddles,
and your steps, like swirling leaves,
grew quick and wary.
My hands always close enough
to catch your breeze.

Worry days drifted and piled,
carried by the ice storm
of your teen fury.
We sank
under its sopping weight.

And after
by years that felt like days
refined by the burn of a climbing sun,
your lean grew lighter.
Together,
we were almost
steady in the balance.

Until today,
you said something
and the scales tipped,
I slid in your direction,
and I wonder how
it felt to you,

like loose bricks, maybe,
under your feet.

FIFTY SOMETHING

Like a bead of water
racing down the shower door,
I was sliding
toward irrelevance.

My fingertips,
thick with lines of absorption,
touched nothing fully.
All seemed gossamer,
a pinch of dandelion seeds
in my grasp.

I prayed,
for relevance,
for purpose,
to matter.

And waited.

And then it came,
like the floods
when the spring downpour
tailgates the
winter snowfall,
purpose deluged my life,
pushing, pulling,
swirling in puddles
of mud and tea-stained leaves
and crystal matter.

I tipped my head back
and soaked up the rain.

KNOWING PRAYER

I used to pray in the language of want
and need,
Morse coding my shopping lists of wishes
to the heavens,
hoping there
among the gilded wonder
someone would fill my order,
plug the gaps in my being
like duct tape on a water raft
grant me the things I need to stay afloat.

I'd kite them up, these petitions,
like water balloons absorbed into heaven,
then wait for the gifts to rain down
washing my life into better-ness.

When the gifts didn't come,
I knew it must have been the fault of my prayers,
too scant
not earnest enough,
overused.
I buckled down and pushed up more.

But then,
after the drought,
I took time to read the Word,
grasped at its message.
Suddenly, I felt light in the pages,
and I knew.

Now my every day is a prayer,
and my prayers have become the heavens

themselves.
Prayers of gratitude
instead of wishes,
now that I can see
it has already rained.

FIBROMYALGIA

Pain, like a careless
house guest,
arrived each morning
at her skin's door,
dropping its bags
and dragging its dirt
across her floor.

It invaded the parlor,
feet upon the table,
anchored at the hearth,
demanding a warm dish
to sooth its burn,
expecting a reply
to its every wish.

By midnight,
it twisted its way
up the long staircase
to claim, of course,
the plushest bed,
scattered its belongings
and bathed instead.

Come one morning,
she was relieved
when she found it gone,
uncovering a towel in the sink,
a sock that strayed,
not caring
that the bed was left unmade.

ON THE MORNING OF YOUR WEDDING

They ask me how I feel
to have my eldest marrying
so young.

I haven't yet thought myself
what the mood will be
as I near our small white church
leaning heavy on your daddy's arm.

But after the music
your bride's careful walk
the Pastor's step forward
we gather together...
let no man tear asunder...

I look at you, my son,
standing solid as a tree
and I become the farmer,
remember the hoeing, the planting,
the praying for rain.
Remember the weeding, the raking,
the staking, the feeding.
Deep in your being
we have sown the seeds of cherish
the soil of honor
the roots of love,

and the feelings run.

They run down the aisle
by the straight caramel pews
by friends and family
by the bountiful years
the meager and sparse ones
all the days lost.

They flow toward the altar
where a sunbeam finds your feet
firmly planted
your arm branching outward
your fingers entwined.

In the final moments
before you say those words
by which you'll till your life,
you glance over your shoulder
and your eyes find mine,
making sure I too am ready
for the harvest.

MAKING ALFREDO

When I can no longer bear the thought
of sending you
heart open and spaghetti thin
into a broken world,
I make Alfredo.
A maestro facing the musicians,
I stand before the cooking pots
and raise my wooden spoons
to cue.

My hand frees wanton tubes of penne
into the simmer,
while steam dances upward—
a formal minuet over the stove.

And I, lost in the misty twirls,
dream potent meals
to protect your bones
from the gnaw of hurt and sorrow,
while the sounds of cooking
echo in hallelujah chorus around me.

Cream and parmesan cheese swirl,
a pinwheel in the saucepan.
Prosciutto crisps and pops
in the fry behind,
sending scented melodies
into the smoke-filled air.

As I drain salted water
through the colander,
I pray your troubles filter too,

life's small joys
resting *al dente* at the bottom.

VINTAGE BEACH SCENE AT WATCH HILL, RI

It wasn't the way
he extended his hand
to tug her to her swollen feet
as if lifting buried treasure
from deep water,

Or the way he tugged her rising shirt
round her back
two-handed
like he had done it all
before,

or how she waddled,
seagull bellied and blistered
toward the water,
pastel cottages like widows
watching from the shore.

The moment he plopped
to their beach blanket.
breezily nesting
while birds salt and peppered
the cerulean sky.

It was the way they paused,
props in a vintage painting
waiting for more love to arrive,
that brought me back
to that very scene
in my own painted life.

WHEN THEIR SISTER LEFT FOR COLLEGE

Three points of your triangle
together on the lawn,
pink disk sailing between you
against the cornflower blue sky.

Three is symmetry,
a polygon,
exactly half a star.

Drop one point,
and you become—
a simple line segment,
lacking direction.

The shortest distance
between three points
has now become a far one.

Isosceles knew
the sum of a triangle,
understood all the angles
grasped the strength in its balance.

When she left,
you two flat-lined,
your faces turned 180 degrees
toward the wind

No longer able to connect.

THINGS A MOTHER PULLS FROM HER PURSE

At lunch, she hears the chorus of her cell phone
and plunges elbow deep
into the crawl space of her purse.

First she pulls some paper, origami-ed by age,
and listens to "I love you"
in the ancient tongue of bubbled hearts.

She grasps at ruminations
caught like hairs across her brush.
Returns to the well of her daughter's crying,
the way her shoulders wilted heavy
under coach's spiteful words;
the sound of tendons snapping
across an open field.

She pulls a crumbled grocery list of
"whys?" long forgotten,
the food cooked and eaten,
the bones now strong.

A prayer book
with names and burdens,
worries she buries deep
in the valleys of her wrinkles
behind her winsome smiles.

She finds dreams wedged in tightly,
hers and theirs,
netted like their locks after a late summer swim,

some loosened, others clipped away.
Reaches deeper still where memories grasp
at the hint of resurrection,
that first faint coo of mama,
sibling giggles from the tub.

Strawberry mouths after a morning
of picking at the farm,
wet baby in a towel nestled on her beach chair at sunset,
the proud shine of Mary Janes on Easter morning.

A stolen win that left him empty,
a Mother's Day poem forgotten at school,
the day they almost saved a bunny from a hawk.

It's all on the table now.

While her cell phone
slinks somewhere across the bottom,
back and forth
her fingers search after it
like a soldier's crawl through the desert.

She finds it only after
the ringing has stopped.

SOME JUNE NIGHTS

we find ourselves
rocker waiting,
asking not the all-seeing sky
but the God who dwells beyond it
for mercy.

Worries of your teenage deeds
shadow themselves in the wave of the flag,
dance in the silhouette of its steadfast pole
cast against the watching moon.

My mind tosses unknowns,
daunting dares, fast cars,
and other teenage platitudes,
into the weight of the night air
until the croak of tree frogs
wrestles them silent.

And then,
when the glow of your headlights
signals another slim escape
from the hungry jaws of
tragedy,

I stare upward
in grateful prayer
for these
trials meant, perhaps, to refine
us both.

SEVENTEEN

"Just late."
That's how you describe our impending arrival
at the ski slopes,
mumbled between scattered song lyrics
floating in the thinning air
and sideways quips that miss your buddy
and ricochet off the window.

Sometimes he answers you
with pauses as deep as the valleys between
the mountains we seek.
If you hear him
through your buzzing ear buds,
you smack him back down.
I giggle as I wind us up and around
the steepness
toward the white-capped peaks
soon to bridle your pent-up verve.

You word-joust each other
some more,
lamenting cramped grasshopper legs and
restless hunger
until
somebody mentions the girl
and suddenly
the talk becomes straight lined
and true.

FAR FROM THE NEST

Love recycles itself
like the trickle and pour
of a crystal stream
over satin rocks.

So, too, my empty arms,
still cold with the ache
of waving you from our nest,
welcome any child
the winds of life might
send my way.

Like a mother hen,
spine strong,
I cluck and corral,
needing to feed them,
warm them,
refill my coop.

Your smiles return
in the rising mist of soup
that warms their bones,
and your wit seeps
as the chatter melts
into conversation
beside the fire.
Sometimes,
I even hear your laughter
echo in the well of their grateful eyes.

At last,
with the full devotion of

a mother hen,
I spread a blanket
and whisper a prayer
that somewhere
a mother
fluffs the feathers
around your tired shoulders
and reminds you of home.

THE SWING OF YOUNG ADULTHOOD

Back then, when time was long
and play was filling,
you'd stretch your hands and feet
toward that vast blue space
that swells above the branches.

Each push I acquiesced
only with the knowing you'd return,
your hair cresting in the wind
like a harried cardinal
or a wandering toupee.

My stomach gripped that tickle
when you sailed away
toward the blue beyond,
one giant leap for me,
one more small tear
in my apron string.

Your legs ran through the air,
your giggle trailing after,
as if forward was
the only way to go.

Now, when time is shorter,
your old swing finds stillness
on its rusted chains,
and your feet reach the ground,
it's a different push
toward a different sky,

still blue with possibility.

This time you dig your heels
into the mulch of your contentment,
and I must push you harder away,
even not knowing for certain
when you'll return.

WRITER'S BLOCK

Last night I dreamt a poet's house
and wandered its spaces
from room to room to room.
As I searched, the house grew and grew
and its contents multiplied.
Rooms of books, piles upon piles,
cosmetics, creams, perfumes, and soap,
pillows and linens
and vases.
A warehouse of imaginings.
And the staircase stretched,
extending itself under my feet
so that my decline took minutes
and minutes more.
I found it on the desk
among notebooks and papers
a poem by Robert Frost,
written on parchment,
never published,
never found.
I perused the manuscript
with hungry eye
feeding my writer's block
with fruitful words.
I framed it with my hands
and read more.
And then, from some portal of my own,
a sound nudged me
back to morning.
Waking on my pillow,
it came to light
the poem was mine now

if I could write it;
it was my dream after all.
I strained to bring the words back up,
to crystallize each lovely line or phrase.
I peered at the fading parchment
but it made no difference at all.

THE AFTERIMAGE

On spring mornings,
I carry my Earl Grey to the porch,
settle myself in the splintering chair,
hear the rattle and roar of the school bus,
don't move.
Resurrect my children's morning natter
in the playful chirrup of the birds.
Decipher snapshots of their smiles
in the afterimage of the sun.
Lean back
and rock.
Rock over the lost days
of waving them off, their earnest smiles
fading in the windowpane,
my prayers buckled into the seat
beside them, Rock over
the late night talks that layered me soft
as they buttressed them.
Rock over the rushing home to fill my lap.
The air is still today,
and the grass' greening
seems to pace the cooling of my tea.
I walk inside to feed the dog.

IF WE COULD JUST DANCE

the way we used to
in that narrow slip
of morning
when the house yawned
and shifted its weight
toward the new day.

you
warm and plump against my chest,
the string of your tiny sleep sack
twirling high above the ground.

If I could just swing you to
my hip
then bounce and jiggle,
your arms flapping
in the breeze of my adoration

just balance
your earnest feet atop mine,
trust my steps
as we rock side to side,
a Frankenstein walk,
the dutiful tock of the metronome
counting lost time.

If we could just dance
cheek to cheek
arms locked straight
jaws set to a kitchen tango
where dinner waits and
homework threatens

to dissolve the moment.
I'd let you lead this time,
dip me toward the earth,
pull me back up,
twirl me beneath the new strength
of your still growing arm
then lean in to kiss my cheek goodbye
before you leave to waltz the world.

ABOUT THE AUTHOR

Julianne Palumbo is a mother, a writer, and a writing encourager. She has published poems, short stories, and essays, and continues to dream about publication of her YA novels-in-verse. She is the author of *Into Your Light* (Flutter Press, 2013) and *Announcing the Thaw* (Finishing Line Press, 2014), poetry chapbooks about raising teenagers. She is the Founder/Editor of *Mothers Always Write*, an online literary magazine about motherhood, and a columnist for *Literary Mama* where she chronicles her recent journey to adopt teenagers out of foster care. When Julianne is not writing, you will find her in the kitchen or the garden or walking the dog.

ACKNOWLEDGEMENTS

The author is grateful to the following journals for publishing her poems first:

"One by One"
> *Mamalode.com*

"Sunset"
> *Rust + Moth*

"Fifty Something"
> *Crack and Spine*

"Knowing Prayer"
> *Ancient Paths*

"On Turning Fifty"
> *The First Literary Review East*

"The Afterimage"
> *Red Bird Chapbooks Weekly Read*

"Something Borrowed"
> *Mothers Always Write*

"Cleaning Day"
> *Mom Egg Review*

"Grown Children"
> *Mothers Always Write*

"Making Alfredo"
> *The Sunlight Press*

"Writer's Block"
> *The Sunlight Press*

"On the Morning of Your Wedding"
> *Mothers Always Write*

www.ingramcontent.com/pod-product-compliance
Lightning Source LLC
Chambersburg PA
CBHW071758080526
44588CB00013B/2293